But I'm Just Saying...
Just Preaching to the Choir

(Real Version Book 1)

By Cheery

ISBN: Softcover   978-0-692-48941-3

This book is dedicated to all the Lost Souls

There is hope

Rest in Peace

Eurydice Davis and Anthony Riley

Table of Contents

Preface/Prologue

The Uplifting

The Questioning

The Disengaging

Just Because

And the Rest

And The End

Reasoning

The Epilogue

Adult Language Not Suitable for Children

I have two versions, one has some profanity and the nice version I either removed or substituted most harsh profane words, neither one has salacious sex but I get my point across one way or another. I use the word nigga, nigger all throughout my work just to let you know. This is no cakewalk by any stretch of the imagination.

(*) Words are substituted or removed.

Funny Disclaimer:

If you read this and think oh I can write better than that then by all means...totally express yourself in whatever way you feel is best.

Preface

I write all the time. I was encouraged while in Middle School to keep a journal and as a matter of fact a teacher, his name was Mr. Reid, funny huh, had the class do a weekly journal entry. He said I needed to learn how to type, my handwriting was terrible. Still is. Also I was told over the years never write the way I speak. Although I am long winded when I talk going all the way around John's barn, but that's not exactly what I mean. My teachers in High School gave me journals and yelled at me when I didn't try. Mrs. M. O. thanks for encouraging me and caring. Ms. D. H. thanks for telling me and another classmate to get it together. I can't mention every last one of them but I love you.

This is just the tip of the iceberg. I continue to write. It is very therapeutic of course just to get your thoughts out even if you just scribble one word.

In this book I have included two songs (Young Man and Young Mizz) I was trying to get someone to perform them years ago. One person had a wonderful, wonderful voice at such an early age, I have no idea what happened to him. Now fast forward to Show Me a Man Pt 1,2 and I Am a MAN. I was trying to get a campaign started. And I made the sincere effort to find someone to perform I Am a MAN and edit or add an entirely different spin to reply to my Show Me a Man lament. I was very angry when I wrote this and still recovering from surgery, my son's father was talking about something that made me upset... I won't say anything else but at least he tried. The campaign was to include me as the woman on the street, small forums on why and where men are as far as the role they play as a man, give men a chance to speak. I was so hurt but I understand. My problem is I have all the plans. I had help from my friend and my cousin to design the logo and from there go to T-shirts. I even talked to Book Man who gave me some good advice. Major fail I was unable to get this campaign off the ground.

No execution, I can't be and do everything. I work, I write. I was thinking about giving up. But with all I have done what would have been the point if I gave up. All of this writing that I have which spans years would just sit there. I have other works that are complete; different genres, different mediums, I have to get this show on the road.

I encourage all who have an idea to put pen to paper. It won't hurt. And if you so please, when you have enough material and after you have done a few things to have your words heard or seen by some different people, put it out there. If you have plans, write them down, take classes, find and get help. It took me this long to do this all the while I was doing other things to get myself out there. This is an easy step now since technology has advanced making things more accessible and affordable.

So I can say I have a book. I have my thoughts out there in the Universe for all who would like to have a peek.

A Huge Thanks

I would like to thank all who encouraged me from grade school up to the present, all who were in my corner, all my teachers who gave a damn and ones that were there that really shouldn't have been because they did not give a damn, RIP Nadine Wright, thanks Donna Ward and RIP Ruth. This is for my son, my nephews and LV. To my friends at work too many to mention here, BB, AM, Sha'C, Day, Neal, MMJ and you CP for constantly saying to me you know you should have been, VC and MW...the poets I have come across they know who they are. Especially Crucial for telling me I need to memorize my poems and I'd better always have something on me if I don't have it in my head. And a whole host of others that I don't know if they would appreciate being mentioned here. I know I didn't ask permission. But what's up to MAR. So don't be afraid, it will be okay, dream, act, write but follow up accordingly. Learn what you need to take you on your way. Trial and error sometimes is how you get there. Have or find some positive support to help along the way if possible.

At the end of the day you have yourself, give yourself a chance and then you can say well at least I tried. And if need be go back and try again. So you do what you can, when you can, while you can.

I sincerely appreciate and thank you for your support and especially C. A. for giving me a chance. And to Amazon for making this part of the process possible.

Again I say Thanks

God knows I have been through a lot and if I didn't have Him this wouldn't be.

Prologue

I found this and thought wow I don't remember writing this at all.
I wrote it a few months after my son was born.

You Mean so Much to Me

Before you came into my life I was not sure of I how I felt about myself

The only thing I knew I was going to do the best I could do (for you)

When I brought you into this world you changed my priorities for life

Yes you are my child to be raised with the love and sacrifice of a parent who really cares

You made me realize there are more important things in this world and gave me the hope I needed to go on

For you my child I will always be there

Because you mean so much to me I will love you unconditionally

Because you mean so much to me I will take care of all your needs

Because you mean so much to me

You will grow up to be healthy, you will be nurtured, you will be well

You will be taught about life until you have learned all there is to know

This knowledge will mature you mind and soul

So when you have children you give love as you have received love

If there is no love God help that child

People loved and cared a whole lot but as you all know today that is not the case. People love and care about themselves a whole lot with no care left for anyone else. Not all People of course but there are way too many more for me and none for you.

So if I say look out for your fellow man of course I may be just "preaching to the choir" because you already do.

The Uplifting

Hmmm

Maybe there are some questions

Some questions that I should have asked

Not knowing that the answers were already there

You know it's good to have questions

Have to know what to ask

There are no dumb questions

Yes there are when it states the obvious

Like you saw me walking down the street

Didn't I just see you walking down the street?

Yeah cuz I walked right past you and said hi

You get the idea

Just make it more complicated

But the absurdity is still there

If I would have known what to ask

Not only that how to ask

And just opened my mouth

Man

So ask questions that need to be asked

Answers open doors

Because you never know

What you may run through

Cloudy

I reached for the sky
But grabbed tree branches instead
Pulled down leaves and seeds

I reached for the sky
Didn't jump high enough
And just stayed in the weeds

I reached for the sky
I couldn't find any other hands
So I put mine down

I didn't reach high enough for the sky
Let my dreams drift away with the clouds

Wasn't thinking when I reached for the clouds for someone else's
dream

Just like you know, that's what I do
I let you step on me then I can step on you

Nope didn't work out that way as it never does

Sometimes people don't step high enough
When they reach for the sky

Or when they do they don't gather enough clouds
Not enough to hold their own
Let alone help someone else

Now all I do is look around

Almost too afraid to reach for anything

Only realizing now I was already in the sky
I just let myself fall to the ground for a long time

Have to start from the very beginning
This time around no reaching for the sky
And grabbing tree branches and pulling down leaves instead

The Questioning

Young Man

I am a Young Man becoming a Grown Man

Don't give me all these issues

I'm not old enough to have these burdens

I want to take my time and see the years ahead of me

All these things making me mature too fast

Coming at me with adult responsibility

I am a Man but a Young Man

So let me be and grow peacefully

I am a Young Man becoming a Grown Man

Don't give me all these issues

Doin' all this shootin' and trickin' ain't even necessary

I have a name, we are individuals but are dealt with fatally

As a Young Man, singled out and left alone

The real story remains untold

I am a Young Man becoming a Grown Man

Don't give me all these issues

Don't label me Gangsta or Baller forcing it

So I am always treated differently

Not to respect me, nor protect me

I battle all day long

I serve a purpose, it's to be conquered

But still I remain strong

I am a Young Man not a grown man
with old man issues

All these issues you put on me, told me to be a man,

Handle it like a man since before I learned to talk

I am a Young Man forced to become an old man

This world is not up to the call I see as a Young Man -
PAY ATTENTION

I'm going to handle these serious issues on my own

I am a Young Man, you gave me all these issues

But I'm going to do what's right for my soul

I will manage as the Man that I have now become

A Young Man forced to become a Grown Man

This is some of the truth that must be told

I Am A MAN

I am a Man

I am not a statistic

I am a Man

Unequivocally chosen into existence

I am a Man

Too many of us bleed upon this earth

I am a Man

Steps unwalked claiming our worth

I am a Man

Take the time to listen

I am a Man

Called for a specific mission

I am a Man

Stop selling myself short, know that God made me
I must stay on course

I am a Man

I am not a conquered entity, I can remain unarmed,

No weapon formed against me

I am a Man

I must take a stand

I am a Man

See great things from our humanity

I am a Man

The future rests with me

I am a Man

Calamity or prosperity I hold the key!

The Disengaging

Shut

Keep your legs closed
Your mouth shut
And your eyes open wide at all times deemed necessary

Keep my legs closed
Nothing can get in
So no worry about anything popping up or coming out

Keep my mouth shut
Words that kill won't escape
Minds won't be overthrown

Feelings will be warm and hearts will be blessed

But sometimes I can't help but think that if I was sleeping with someone
Some of the things I want to do would get done

This someone told me it would take a year to completely know someone physically

You know the compatibility test
Which is entirely based on sex

Okay so what am I gonna get out of it
Don't mean to sound selfish, that's not my intent

I had another someone tell me, well, you get me

I was like

What!!! I can have all of you? Really...

Muthafucka please, dicks run a million

I don't want yours or you since you put it like that

Oh wait a minute let me break it down into terms you can understand

Nigga

Treat me like your best watch you always have by your side

Look at me when you need time

Talk about me and make comparisons with other thugs
About how good I am and that my look is good

Hold me out for everyone to see, caress me and cover me

Put me up at night or carefully lay me right next to you

Might reach out for me in the middle of your dreams to see if I'm still there

When you wake up in the morning after taking a piss and
Maybe brushing your teeth you look for me

Look at me

I see the care in your eyes every time

Very proud and confident in your choice of expression
As you step out of the door day by day with me

See how you treat your piece
But it only meets one primary goal
And that is my basic need.

Love Lost

It's okay

Woman: I will never have someone to fall back on

Man: I will never have someone lean on me

I will never have someone to cuddle

I will never have someone to hug

No snuggle, no warm feelings, no back rubs

From me to you or from you to me

Because we never found each other

It is unfortunate but we never met

Time is coming to an end

When all of my energy will be gone

Search and we will not find

What we need from any other

I was here

You were there

We were

Cruising in and out of other people's lives

We are there and unrecognized

Too bad we aren't programmed magnets

We seek and are destroyed

I know if I were with you

If it were permanent

I would fuck you in a different way

Never Married

Well I have never been married

Ain't gonna get married

Don't care about marriage

Marriage makes a home

My home is almost over

My kid will be on their own

Starting a new home

I never planned right

Never really took it seriously

Once with the father

Marriage was considered but never completed

Now my son is almost grown

I know he sees all the mistakes I've made

Somewhat trying my best to give some type of stability

Not the kind I had...

No real dad he didn't know how, no house to call a home

No room of my own...

Trying to hold onto something

Let me hold onto my kid...

Held on a little too tight but he alright

I'm not and since I never planned

I don't need a man to make a family

But I did the best with what I had

Married

Not being Married is a crime

I am hurt everyday being alone

No huge loving family to support me

No one to step in and fill the shoes

Where my husband should be

All of these baby Mommas

Oh I'm a man tho

Take care of yourself

Choose one to be with

Not being Married is a crime

Having kids one of them there and two here

All with different mommies

Children suffer

Women suffer

You suffer the most

That is your fault

All that child support

Show Me a Man (Part I)

Show me a man

It's been a while since I seen one

I mean besides the ones that I know which are few

I see a wolf in man's clothing

Show me a man

Are there really any besides the one I know of

From what I can tell these wolves in man's clothing

They don't want to take full responsibility or don't know how

A blind eye hears everything

What a poor excuse

I will accept if you have a mental defect

Deficient due to improper nurturing

Weak genes

But they having babies

Only caught up in the act but not the actual product

Show me a man

I can't count on one hand

Real man

None helped to raise me

But some were in my family

A few uncles that I was close to

Hmmm

A few friends as well

They range in age from the very young to the very old

Only counting the ones in which I communicate

None of any that I've only slept with

Man just because you got your dick in your hand

Punk ass bitch

Try making a house a home

Try taking the long road

Instead of dropping out of school

Selling drugs or hanging in the streets

I don't want to hear you ain't a man

Don't know the pressure of what one of you must endure just to maintain

If you so good at being bad, doing wrong and going out of your way to wreck havoc

You stupid motherfucker

Do the opposite

The straight and narrow to the horizon every damn day

When you fail miserably at your God given responsibilities

Don't complain when people call you animals, dogs, pussies to name a few

If you don't understand I know can't teach you how to be a man

But why am I put in the position of being one

Me because of the half-ass you call dad

AT

All together

I like to see men with their kids

Never mind her

Get your kids if you can

Never mind him

Let him see his kids

Make sure your kids are not harmed

Cause like it or not they know what's going on

Get old enough and will start to tell

Mom, Dad if that's how they feel

Or call you by your government name

Either way you will find out

If you hurt or if you helped

The lament I don't need a man

Of course you don't

That's your choice

But if that man is a good influence

Don't decide for your kids

Because then the streets get the chance

Street life living Street code

Show Me a Man (Part II)

Show me a man

Biologically you are packed and carrying

No doubt you are male

Physically embodying every sense of that word

You are a male

Now man what are you doing for you

I see you out there

Fighting (hunting) that's all within your traits

But the problems arise with who and why you fight

Fellow man, fellow woman, God

No one is your friend

You are at war against your very self

Every time you smoke

And over drink and take pills like candy

War against everybody

No peace in your mind

After the civil rights movement instead of furthering ourselves
We parted like the Red Sea

No longer keeping each other company

We made it

Got into all the schools, access to everything
Of course there are roadblocks set up nothing is ever that easy

But instead of building beyond the obstacles you added to them

Dumb ass

Another kind of slavery

This time it's you enslaving yourself

Your choice of slave that you choose to be today

Show me a man

And I will show you a slave

Not a slave to the good things that will lift up man

Nope slave to the guns, cars, sneakers, clothes, sex, self-gratification, street credibility, praise

He didn't do all that he could so his son could have a better life

He didn't do all that he could because he was jealous

Not clearly thinking ahead- How SELFISH!!!

Whaaat!!!

I Hurt

Hurt on the outside

Hurt on the inside

Hurt from the outside reverberates through me

Almost to my soul

I Hurt

I wear it like a coat I don't particularly care for

Hurt so much on the inside

Hurt so much it's thick like a halo

Why Hurt >

People

Place

Thing

I saw it

I became

Hurt lies there and I'll be damned if I can't escape it

What Hurt >

You think God ain't near

How Hurt >

Grow in it

Hate

Unoriented

Running

Terrify

Who Hurt >

We

No beginning but oh, it will end!

Just Because

?

My life has been borrowed

Time to give that shit back

I mean really I tried to take care of it

As best I can...

God giveth and he taketh away

I never asked one way

Take it back it sucked being here

I know I tried to right all wrongs

Be right as right can be

Still see people doing wrong

Prosperity never gifted me

Don't care now what happens to them

If I stop to question it will never make any sense

Doing all the wrong in the world

But still doing fine

It's okay because soon it will be

Your time

We cross paths every so often

I wish you no harm so nothing will happen

Not because I care but because I call myself

A Christian and know that all vengeance is mine

saith the Lord

So I don't want to be nowhere in sight

when you get yours

I Like the ATTENTION

He all up in my face

How does that make me feel

Well, wanted

I want to be America's Most Wanted

No, really I want to be his most wanted

He sees me so should I give up this easily

Well here I am

But I'm about to beats and rhymes my black ass on out of here

What do I have to lose

If I let him stay

Today my face

Tonight some other place

maybe

I am confused

Just the thought makes me cringe

But I like the ATTENTION

The feeling is like no other

And cannot be bought or sold

Sex is My Money / My Money is Sex

Now I'm not wild
but that's my style
it suits me

When I get laid
my bills get paid

Sex, that is my form of currency

It's fair exchange
No free trade

See I gets mine

Now you look down
I see you scowl
Umm what's the funny face for

See close your eyes
While you up in me

Well I get down
When he around

Don't like my way
yeah
It's okay

I don't waste a fuck

My livelihood is all wrapped up

Prepaid

As long as I can spread and smile

My legs open wide
No worries today because they all fade

Is misery your experience?

Let's get it straight

My destiny is made

No time to be sad or
should I say unglad

You right there
and
I'm right here

We don't have to click
but we can connect

If on you what I need is found
then those are the grounds
of fuckability

Sex is my money
You are used for currency
Sex is my money/my money is sex

Don't like it well that's just too bad
Don't like it then don't touch me

Hos= 1min

Why are people hos

Is that too much to ask

Smiling and grinning

Fucking and playing

All day

Family just disintegrating

Mind games

That was the plan all along

Destroy, Destroying, Destroyed

Everything

Don't get mad if he cheating on you

Don't get mad if she cheating on you

Because it's okay to screw

All hypocritical and hyperethical

Now you want to say something

Well keep your fucking mouth shut

Yes I mean that literally and fig YUH RAHH TIVE LEE

Bending over backwards

Doing flips and shit

Sure it feels good

But complain about the consequences

Look, whose life are you ruining

Don't be a ho dummy

Just say no to being a ho

Right?

Right (nod your head)

Right

Not Me

You are well done now

Over cooked

You are burning, well was burnt before and didn't learn

Smoking first

Now you are FIRE! Carrying a whole bunch of
STIs known to man

Got one treated and went on like nothing happened

Got number two thought that scar was gonna be permanent

Three was a little something "everyone" gets called
Chlamydia

You passed that on to quite a few people men and women

Four well stuck around and isn't going anywhere

Those sores and blisters are yours to wear

They are down there and up here /\

Don't scratch because you might get them there

That should have been enough

But no you were going for the gusto

Now you got the big HIV

Think that's where you were headed
all along with no condom usage

Didn't care when you got it
just said oh well one of the side effects
of slipping it in

Can't sacrifice the immense feeling of pleasure from skin on skin

Wonder what I'm gonna do now

Oh wait I can just take some pills

Sounds easy enough

A pill everyday

And now I'm thinking because the pills aren't working

Now I look back across the scales

How I didn't weight out the circumstances
because I was like who cares...

Too late now because I've been touched by HIV

It can happen to you just like I let it happen to me

Ranting Random Thought

If you didn't let that fuck get in the way
we'd still be friends today

PArty Now

Party now because you won't later

Party till you die

Apocalypse

While you were drinking

Yelling and hollering

Like there is no tomorrow

There will be no tomorrow

Apocalypse now

Days will never be the same

Find your Bible

Run and hide

Fade to black

Where is your party at

You were warned

Party till you die

You were already dead

Now look at hell

Make Old Straight

What happened!

I am old before my age

Damn I played too hard

Partied too long

I can't believe the aches and pains

What happened!

Wrinkles, wrinkled everywhere

 I can't reverse this

Take back all the play hard and long

Too late

Just need to make way

Make things straight

Soon you will make a visit

It will be to my grave

Shed no tears

Only pray people see

As they look at you

And now at me

Because here is where I lay

Can't change the state of things

Only the effect of my grave

My grave can change things

When people see

I was young but looked old

They are all aged

And the Rest

Stay on Top

I have a decision to make

I should have did this a long time ago

Things are just starting to fall in place

Dumb thinking

Can't get no place

I should have been focused

Future based

Not willy nilly

Mind in space

Now I don't know what to do

Something I should

If I had to leave

No problem for him

Just leave me high and dry

Like we were never friends

I need to look at it from that perspective

He does all this stuff for me

He does too much for them

They take advantage

Maybe so do I

He guilt trips about all of us

They too old to be trippin him

And they have spouses...

I have myself

Dumb dumbs

I guess I'm one added with those two

Should have just kept it moving

He should be fine

Just surround himself with his kids' time

So there you have it in a nutshell

My dilemma

Self-made crime

Capital N-word by Design

I HATE Philadelphia

Because it is on the corner
Not even the top part but the bottom of the state
But I like my area because it is convenient
A straight shot by train or bus to work
But just because it is convenient doesn't make it right

Niggers are convenient cuz that's what I see
When I say Niggers I am all inclusive
Not color but how you act is what matters to me
Although Black is a lot more plentiful
If you don't know what I mean then it's probably you

There is no excuse to behave in such a manner
Disregard etiquette and be out of bounds with respect
Fuck education, I'll make it how I make it

I'm like whatever, keep it over there
Don't impose upon me and mine
Soon as you do
The problem that you caused me is gonna be a bigger one for you

See

That's because I can be Nigger too
Don't like to be like that because number one I'm Black
Known all too long
Cuz Nigger is our main name I try not to claim

Our predecessors died over it but without choice
Today we die over and over
Just dropping and I know why
Can't blame anyone but Niggers because we know how to get ours
But it's all wrong we got ours after the civil rights movement

Today

Civil- Which is how Niggers don't know how to act

Rights- Don't care about anyone's except their own. I got the right to take what I think should be mine even if it is yours

Movement- All over the fucking place, Niggers is everywhere! Niggers are convenient

BSU

This is a piece about total and utter
absolute nonsense
I wonder how people can be so deep in
talking their shit
So much nothing coming out of their mouths
to fill my ears

Makes me cringe
I look at them talking, talking, talking nothing
but shit not funny or good but nonsense

Will you
Please Shut Up!!

But if I tell them that I would be wrong
How can you tell people who
when they move their lips and
nothing comes out to be quiet

Talking I mean speaking should be a
privilege.
If what you say is bullshit and
not the good kind
your jaw should automatically
lock open so someone can stuff
knowledge down your throat!

So no one would dare look at you
with pleading eyes to cease existence
Knowledge so great that when you open
your mouth the sun shines and the stars come out
That way no matter what if it's night or day
what you speak will at least look bright

After I read it I tossed the 5x10 index card onto the floor.

So Sushi

Some Such Shit as the conversation overflows

Manners and common sense
are lost these days

Oh you can find a sprinkle of it here and there

Manifestations of Thank you, Please, let me step and or move
out of the way

I don't have 3 kids by 3 different men,

I don't have 6 baby mommas and let me get that for you,
have since gone asunder

Some Such Shit

It's good to have your nipples pierced and your clit

No one is entirely good or evil

Mothers don't know how to balance it out with the good
being way better than the evil

Fathers disappear and pop up and that's if they do
whenever they feel like it

Some Such Shit

Peaches: I'm bipolar

Judy: Oh, are you

Peaches: Yeah
I don't take medication for it
now that my situation is better and I stop
being around assholes or just stop
letting myself be privy to their bullshit problems

I'm good.

Judy: It's something that you say that because I suffer
from major depression I used to think about killing
myself all the time

Just tired of everything.

Peaches: Oh wait girl you can't be thinking about killin yourself
you young black in America

Some Such Shit

Walk down the street and get shot, unwanted, involuntary
suicide perpetrated by who is black on black

Hair is very, very popular and more than likely will always be very popular in the Black Community, it's a natural thing now but people still put emphasis on big, long, thick hair and say "good hair". Damned if that ain't some old timey brain washed crap. I frowned up when someone said my hair was nice because it felt soft. Can I manage it that's all I care about; is it manageable meaning what can I do with what I have on top of my head so it can be maintained, if I want to keep what's on top of my head.

There is hair, different types and colors, locs or loose. I have had problems and I say problems because I could not and still can't get it right. From the horrific oh so unprofessional experiences with salon owners and hair stylists over the past six years to me messing up my own hair by mixing products (I stripped it). Oh yes I used to think that wavy, shiny hair was "good" and looked better back in the day. There are some styles I can't wear that I like because I need bone straight hair etc. There are ways around that... My hair right now is on its way out. I wrote Nap Back when natural (unpermed/unpressed) was not the trend like it is now, in 2015, in the Black community. There is some consciousness that goes with it but not much because I still hear the term "good hair" and there is an emphasis on length. Let it go, it's just hair, if it is clean and looks good on you then by all means. But of course boundaries exist based on profession. I don't want to see anyone's (every and all ethnicities, race, creed did I leave a term out) "big" hair when I am in a health setting or food setting. It is NOT appropriate. Because you know hair (synthetic included) can and does shed and can land anywhere. Nets and caps can only cover/protect but so much and protocols are in place for a reason.

Hair and mine is coarse…I have a love hate relationship with my hair due to my own experience not because of texture but can't separate it entirely. I want a fro. I can't now but I will eventually and that's when I won't care about attention. If I am able to or if it matters I will elaborate on that statement sometime later on down the line. Blend in sista, blend in…nope. All that money and not to mention time can be best used elsewhere…there can be arguments about small businesses etc. that benefit. Exorbitant that discussion is moot with some folk.

See this is the only piece that has an intro so that just goes to show. Here Hair Hear now…we are not our hair. But the intense focus and scrutiny at times suggests otherwise. Whatever you have or don't have on your scalp, hair texture: it's not "good", "nice" or that other term "bad", it just is and that is not a matter of opinion it is fact.

Nap Back

All my life we had to fight!

I fought naps and they fought back

I combed, I spray dyed, I fried but those naps kept coming back

I pulled, I pressed, I curled

Those naps came back and said we ain't takin this no more

I cut, I permed and those naps said uh huh

We'll teach you we not coming back any more

People fought my kind of hair for a very long time

I fought off and on and mostly tried to hide
with hats, wigs, braids, an occasional weave

Those naps crept back and peaked up between plaits,
poked out from under wigs and surprised people when
they came out from hiding through weaves

Damn I'm so tired of these naps and fightin them

I guess they got tired too

They started losing, giving up, breaking off and
filling up trash bags
Just jumpin right in

So I am going to stop hiding and binding my naps
I am so fed up, don't know what to do

All the attention they create

Might as well let them take CENTER STAGE

Those naps said that's RIGHT!!!
CENTER STAGE sounds GREAT

Because naps know if they are gone for good
You'd sit and wish you had a single nap back

My naps scared me so bad a couple times I cried

Now I have learned to embrace them because
Bottom line is these naps are mine
they grow on top of my head

Who am I trying to impress

Because these naps,
well as hard as I tried are not going to entirely disappear

You know

They grow everywhere

But it's okay though
How I feel about my hair is all in my head

I shouldn't feel bad
But one more peep out of you naps that make me pause

I will electrocute YOU BITCHES

POOF HAIR BE GONE!!!!

———

Switch

Rows and rows of columns line the platform
Why they are red and green I cannot imagine
One walks to the edge
While one just stands there
They cross paths
Swing Switch Swag
One waltzes down singing at the top of his lungs
Swing Switch Swag
He walks to the other side

She sat slightly slouched in her seat. Head tilted to the side, mouth slightly ajar. Sound asleep on the mostly empty train car.

ANOMALY

No one needs my life.

Her hair was in an uproar. It calmed down only after she washed and conditioned it. Sections of hair were apportioned off and two strand twists done capturing a short doo perfectly.

Ami could not sleep. She always thought if she had a warm body to exercise with during those nights, which were often, she would be fine. She didn't think the man would mind sex every other night as long as he was able. Since that was not going to happen she settled for memories of touches the best and the worst lovers. Lover what a misnomer. No love involved there.

Managing to operate on four hours of sleep a day, Ami was all smiles every time she stepped onto the floor of her job. Her co-workers had no clue that she hated that fucking place. Would never really complain unless they got on her nerves and they could be anyone. Anyone directly related to her duties as a case manager working with elderly individuals. Seniors with disabilities, some worked, a few only needed someone to manage their affairs. She loved her clients.

At the end of the day she makes her way through multiple doors. First one, then two, then three, four doors all the way to the outside world. A nice wind smacks her face, that headache intensifies. A short walk to the train pass the bums and hangers on. Descend the stairs to the subway. Pay the fare, a single swipe on top of the box. Go through the turnstile. Descend more stairs. Wait on the funky platform with some of the most quietest people. Strange when no one knows each other and even if it's a large crowd it is virtually silent. Almost makes up for the ride home. The D train enters the tunnel and comes to a hell of a screeching stop in front of the platform. Damn get the breaks fixed. Shit! People get up from the benches, move forward from walls and take their places. They frame the doors. People exit. Get stared down by a few bystanders if they look good or weird. Some people just bust off the train and bump into folk. Some passengers already on the train, like asses, like to stand in front of the door and not move. Some people start to board even while people are still coming out. Rude, simple ignorant bitches.

Ami boards the train after everyone else has entered through the doors. Finds a nice seat with her back against the wall. No one is sitting across from her blocking the view out the window of the tracks. This car, surprisingly, is not too crowded. She looks to her left and spots something.

Ami mumbles under her breath, "Why is this fool sitting here with a cereal bowl and spoon lookin like oatmeal crust left on the sides and bottom. Hmmm very interesting and very strange."

He is not well dressed, just some dude looking a little disturbed.

Ami almost doses off and with half-mast eyes stares across the aisle out the window as the train flies past the steel columns. It slows down to a stop. Doors open, people board. This is the express train. The doors close, now on the move, it picks up speed.

Ami stares out the window, still no one sits across from her to obscure the nice view as the train speeds thru the tunnel. She sees the platform on the other side, a blur of people, walking, standing on the platform as the train whizzes past.

Lights, another platform. Gordy Park, the train slows down very nice and convenient as it passes thru the tunnel providing a clear view of the platform. Ami stares across the tracks with full panoramic view, she eyes a guy walking on the platform toward where the front of the train comes to a stop. Ami sees another guy that looks similar to the first guy. Just like school kids wearing backpacks or book bags is what we called them back in my day, everyone looks the same.

There are three passes and one stop and then Ami will disembark. Ami closes her eyes for what seems like eons as the train begins to pick up speed again. Another station platform, Barcone, comes into view. Ami allows her gaze to set on and track a guy walking in the same direction as the guys she noticed at Gordy Park. With the exception, well this man has on a suit. Geez Ami wishes she had binoculars because she could tell from way across the tracks that this man looked good. Oooo weee.

Terry Station. Ami exits the train. A man in a shiny, not cheap shiny, but expensive shiny business suit walks toward her. He is headed for the revolving bars to make his getaway off the platform. She gives him the once over. Then stares him dead in the eye. He can't tell because Ami always sports a pair of Ray Bans.

Ami thinks out loud, "He looks just like that other guy. Two suits on the same day and one actually gets off at the same stop as me. What are the odds of that. This is rush hour. There should be a million suits but yet there is only one. Rush hour morning or noon, early or late I never see a business suit at this stop but I see plenty of women. But I happen to see one today. So what does that say, it's an anomaly."

Ami wishes one day that one of those suits will be waiting as she is walked down the aisle to greet him and become permanent or what is supposed to be a permanent roommate.

That's not going to happen. There will be no one to walk her down the aisle. There will never be an aisle to walk down.

Why because she is a black female in her forties whose time has run out. If she wants to get married to a black man that's not going to happen in 2015 or ever. Too many are gay, in jail, got drama, too many kids, too many girlfriends, are just hos, don't care, don't want a family, jealous, no ambition, want someone to care for them, misplaced priorities, on drugs, selling drugs, are fools, punk ass, abusive, and don't want to change and this is acceptable.

Television is not helping, all the sophisticated glorified hos. That is not the image I want thrust upon me. Don't care if you fucking Presidents and all the CEOs, COOs of all the top companies in the world. I want my own husband not someone else's.

I gave you a chance before you gave yourself a chance now shut the fuck up...

Ami wonders why she feels this way, is it because she has mental issues.

The odds are greater that a Black Man will get shot than get married.

I Take Multiple Tours

At the end of the trip last STOP
Dreams Achieved

I am getting on the take me to my goals. The End is Near Bus
Company. Route E: Buses run every 20 minutes.

I am on this bus, I get off at 25 to take a tour of Lance what a whack job. I run back to the stop and see another bus and get on. I get off again to take a tour of Keye nice and talented very young, whore to the core. I am hurt. He drops me off at the bus stop. I wait and see another bus I get on. I get off again to take a tour of Jamil. He was nice and strong and very, very interesting but also very wrong. I ran around in circles like an ass for him. I just couldn't get enough. I am very reluctant but I walk back to the bus stop. Jamil picked me up again and let me out. So here I wait for another bus. This one I get on and say I'm staying on. I almost died a couple of times I need to keep my legs closed and stress levels even. I cannot let whatever is outside affect me in a negative way no matter what it is. Stay on the bus. Nope I am on the bus but I get off again because someone asked me a question, Trey this time around. I had to oblige the conversation. I didn't know all of these things were going to happen. He dropped me off at the bus stop. I saw a bus I didn't get on. I went back to him. He dropped me off at the bus stop. I stayed there for a while, he came and picked me up. He dropped me off. I didn't get on. He asked did I need a ride. Yes please. I should have stayed and waited for that bus. I am riding with him. He knows I need to get back on that bus. His life has been detoured and re-routed permanently to only God knows where. Had I known ahead of time what I was getting into or where I was getting at I would have stayed on that bus. I am hurt again. I am going to get back on that bus and this time I'm going to stay on it until I reach Dreams Achieved. I cannot believe I let myself stay off for this long. Oh he helped me with the times but I didn't know everything about him but what I did know was counter reacting to my soul. See he is just like me in some ways very nice and a special sweet. I have to leave him now for my sake and if he came back to me all that stuff he had going on he would have had to change. Before I get off the bus again to be entirely with him. I told him you know I love you. He said I didn't, if I did I would be with him and do what he wants me to do. I said to him you misconstrued it. I do love you and you will realize how much later on down the road.

Not Expatiating

You may have low expectations

But I'm just living this low expectating life

Getting nowhere and fast

Having nothing

And doing the same

I'm where I'm supposed to be

Not where I want to be

Right now my low expectating life is hectic

It's like a roller coaster ride gone bad

Hold on with all your might

Because a ride it is

Not always nice

Living a low expectating life

There is no advantage

The goal is to get past it

Starting, living the high life

Whatever that may be

Would be great if it were God

Some seek money

Like they want to become money

Their whole life is one big commodity

I just live a low expectating life

But I'm not a low life

And The End

TTYL

I don't see brown...
Oh really how nice and convenient
So what is it that you see?

My skin is that hue
Do you see through me

Ignore me
Hate yourself

Somehow I am of a lesser kind
Just doesn't and will not for the life
Ever ever make any sense

You don't see brown
Well one day you did
That's when you decided
To not care

All browns or just certain kinds
Ones like yourself

Drown in doubt
Afraid to move

Eaten from the inside out
Attacked from the outside in

Where is your spirit at
Did it dissipate
Was is sucked from you
So to whom are you beholden

Fallin Apart

But I wasn't fighting anything

I was making sure I was ok from just simply living

My body is I believe falling apart

I'm not even that old

Damn sure don't look it

But my body claims the way I act

Old

Nothing else should be wrong

I have stuff messed up since I was born

Every other year it might be the same

Or it might be something new

I am tired I can't handle

Not even that

Want

Another attack

I should be in perfect health

Haven't I suffered enough

Apparently not

Cursed upon this earth

But as long as I smile

And have an understanding

I know that this is only temporary

When God comes back His will be done

This hurt will be null and void

Young Mizz

Intro
Excuse me Young Mizz
Why are you walking alone with this sad look in your eye?
You are too beautiful to be under a cloud
So walk with me on this day and I will open up rays of shine to take the sad away.

He says:
Hey Young Mizz
It's raining and you don't have an umbrella--
Here, you can have mine

She says:
We can share

Verse
Can we spend some time and hang out--
Not your place or mine
We'll go and see some sites

I got a Young Mizz
I needed a Young Mizz to chill out with

Can I walk you home, hold your hand,
Catch a hug, maybe later a kiss
I want you to walk with me in my life

Weeks go by
You are so sweet, not uptight
This is fine

I got a Young Mizz
I needed a Young Mizz to chill out with

We grow closer
Just know you're around is (oh) so
Nice
Always talk, play alright
You are walking with me in my life

Months go by, side by side
We mature Young Mizz and Young Man

Then we had one big fight
What did you say
No I care or I'll be there
Just get out

Please come back, let's make this right
You can be with me
Keep the bull out of our lives

Hey Young Mizz

I'm so glad you came back\through my life
A more perfect love we could never possess

Because you touched my soul and we became mates

Together we are Young Man and Young Mizz.

Reasoning

What child says I want to commit suicide when I grow up...
But a series of events, combined with the love or lack thereof, state
of mind and how one feels, the circumstances in which they find
themselves, leads up to that single final act

Epilogue:

Two ships passed in the night

Moved like pieces on a checker board

About the Author

Cheery continues to write and live on the East Coast.

What's the word, you can contact her at Cheeryfiles@gmail.com